The White Tower at the Tower of London was built as a fortress-palace by William the Conqueror. Work began in 1078 and was completed 20 years later in the reign of his son, William Rufus. The Tower is London's oldest royal palace.

Above: A Yeoman Warder of the Tower of London. The warders are familiarly known as "Beefeaters", a nickname probably derived from the rations doled out to them long ago. A menagerie was once housed at the Tower but today only ravens remain. Like the warders, the birds are considered residents and receive a daily ration's allowance.

Right: A Chelsea Pensioner. King Charles II founded the Royal Hospital, Chelsea, for veteran soldiers in 1682. The three-cornered hat and distinctive coat worn by the 400 in-pensioners is similar to the uniform worn by soldiers in the early 18th century.

Previous page: *A mounted trooper of the Household Cavalry.*
The trooper belongs to the regiment known as the Blues and Royals
who, with the more senior regiment of Life Guards,
serve as the sovereign's bodyguard. They escort Queen Elizabeth II

on State occasions and form the Queen's Guard at the
Horse Guards building in Whitehall every day.
The Blues and Royals wear dark blue tunics and have red plumes on
their helmets; the Life Guards have red tunics and white plumes.

Above: *Trafalgar Square is in the heart of London and all distances from the capital are measured from the statue of Charles I at the top of Whitehall. The National Gallery occupies one side of the square; the church of* St Martin-in-the-Fields *is on the corner diagonally across from the equestrian statue of George IV; and South Africa House lies on the east side.*

CONTENTS

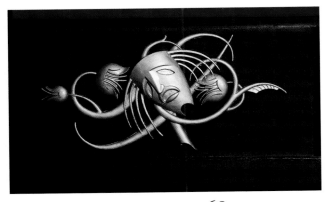

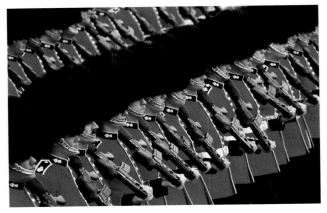

Opposite: HM Queen Elizabeth II and HRH Prince Philip, Duke of Edinburgh.

Left top: Tower bridge.

Centre: The Thames flowing through the centre of London.

Below: A pre-war London "bobby" gives directions and Big Ben.

Right: Piccadilly Circus (late 1930's).

INTRODUCTION

London is one of the world's great cities. Older than Amsterdam, Berlin or Moscow and roughly contemporary with Brussels, Geneva and Lisbon, it has been taking shape for 2,000 years. The Roman legions of the Emperor Claudius, looking for a place to ford the River Thames, built a bridge at Southwark in AD 46 and settled on the north bank close to the site of present-day London Bridge. Within a few years, "Londinium" had become, according to Tacitus, "a celebrated centre of commerce".

During their 400-year occupation the Roman invaders built a forum, a governor's palace, temples and merchants' houses, enclosing their 330-acre settlement inside a great defensive wall. This area grew to just under a square mile, and is known

as the City of London. It is the oldest and smallest of the 33 administrative districts that make up today's metropolis and, paradoxically, the most modern to look at.

To the west of the City or the "Square Mile" lies Westminster, the royal and political heart of England for 1,000 years. A younger but no less important district, it was designated a city in its own right in 1900, a fact that frequently confuses visitors who do not immediately realise that London comprises two cities and 31 boroughs.

London has no logical pattern. A lack of symmetry has resulted in a patchwork urban sprawl. Parts of the wall that enclosed the Roman city are still visible beside towering 20th-century concrete and glass structures. The straight roads of Londinium and the medieval cat's-

cradle of winding alleys survive in outline only because commercial considerations dictated that the City be rebuilt hurriedly after the Great Fire of 1666 reduced 436 acres to a mass of rubble and smouldering timbers. Well-proportioned houses of brick and stone replaced the half-timbered medieval dwellings but these, in turn, and their Georgian and Victorian successors, were destroyed during the Second World War. Almost half of the churches designed by Sir Christopher Wren, the architect of St Paul's Cathedral, in the aftermath of the Great Fire were saved or reconstructed, and today in a City where God met Mammon and lost, their graceful spires are an elegant contrast to an increasing number of soaring office towers.

In Westminster houses sprang up around the Benedictine abbey founded beside the royal palace by Edward the Confessor in 1065, and by the late-13th century regular meetings of parliament and legal courts had established Westminster as the country's principal seat of power. In medieval days the surrounding area was mostly countryside. Small villages occasionally interrupted the farms, forests and hunting grounds that lay to the north and west. This land was gradually encroached as the Court began to expand, and a shortage of accommodation in the City after the Great Fire saw houses go up on meadows now covered by the shops and houses of the West End. The royal hunting grounds were preserved and St James's Park, Green Park, Hyde Park, Kensington Gardens and Regent's Park remain legacies of London's rural past.

From the late Middle Ages until the beginning of the 20th century London was the largest city in the western world, and the most populous. The City was the centre of the financial life of the nation and the Thames was busier than any Continental river. London had become the most important trading city in Europe during the reign of Queen Elizabeth I, and prosperity brought a rapid expansion. Later, the Industrial Revolution and the growth of the British Empire increased its position of eminence, and the population, which topped one million inhabitants in 1800, had multiplied to more than 4,500,000 by the end of the century.

Office space was needed in the City and Westminster. Wealthy merchants had begun to follow the example of the nobility and bought country houses on the fringes of London. People who had once lived and worked in the same premises moved to outlying towns. Small villages were swallowed up by the expanding city. Housing estates mushroomed beside railway lines that cut through fields on the outskirts of the city. The Underground tunnelled its way into Essex, Kent, Middlesex and Surrey. The metropolis ate into the countryside and by 1965 Greater London had grown to 1,580 square kilometres that today stretch from Heathrow Airport in the west to Ockenden in Essex and from Potters Bar in the north to Coulsden in Surrey, the whole area encircled by a notoriously busy motorway, the M25. Inside this boundary the population, which peaked at 8,600,000 at the outbreak of the Second World War and subsequently dropped to 6,500,000, has recently started to rise again and 7,000,710 lived in London in 1995.

Each of London's 33 districts has a historic past, but in a fast-changing world being taken over by technological advancements, each has had to adapt and acknowledge the need to prepare for the third millennium. Nowhere is this more evident than in the City where the occasional old building sits a little incongruously beside a contemporary architect's homage to a new concept and new materials. In the last 50 years the Square Mile has been rebuilt almost entirely. Banks and commercial buildings are continually being demolished to make way for state-of-the-art offices equipped to cope with the electronic revolution that will enable the City to remain pre-eminent among the financial trading centres of the world. A quarter of a million people travel daily into the City. Fewer than 5,000 inhabit it.

The modern Londoner resides in one of the other boroughs, most of which have fine parks and gardens. London is renowned for its open spaces. Five of the royal parks are in Westminster or Kensington, and many of the squares created in the 17th and 18th centuries are made up of terraced houses overlooking a central lawn bordered by trees and flowers.

In outer London many of the mansions built by rich merchants as country homes have been torn down or adapted to another use but the estates often remain as parkland maintained by local councils. Ealing, for instance, has more than 120 public parks; Croydon can claim 3,000 acres of green land; and two-fifths of Richmond's 14,000 acres are open spaces. Common land, too, has been preserved: Blackheath, Hounslow Heath, Epping Forest, Enfield Chase or Wimbledon Common are enjoyed by local residents. Deserted acres along the once-commercial River Lea have been transformed into the 23-mile Lee Valley Leisure Park with hides for birdwatching, a farm, reservoirs for sailing, a lido, a cycle circuit and a huge sports centre. "The parks are the lungs of London", said the Georgian prime minister William Pitt. They are London's pride.

The River Thames, the city's main highway for more than 1,900 years, was the principal source of London's wealth. Its position, close to the sea made London a port of international importance, and for centuries all international shipping used quays downstream from London Bridge to load and unload goods. A point of suffocation was reached around the year 1800: so many ships lay at anchor in the river that it was possible for a man to walk from bank to bank without touching water. The answer to the congestion lay in the creation of wet docks. These were dug out between the Tower of London and the mouth of River Lea, near Canning Town, and continued to operate until well into the 20th century. But the introduction of containers and supertankers and the growth of air travel saw the decline of the once-flourishing docks and the last dockyard gates closed finally in 1970.

Today the great docks are silent; the Thames is no longer a commercial river busy with tall sailing ships. Instead they have become waterways for yachts, floating restaurants and watersports enthusiasts. Pleasure boats meander along the river, passing stately buildings and modern apartments instead of warehouses. Wharves where cargoes of mundane essentials and exotic goods were unloaded are now lined with smart new houses and office blocks. The Docklands, once workaday areas hemmed in by high, grim walls, are alive again. They are vibrant places to live and work.

London has a fascinating history and the past is always present even though the city has changed greatly over the centuries. Evidence of earlier days breaks through, sometimes hidden behind modern buildings, often tucked at the end of quaint alleys. Seek it out and know that restoration and renovation keep the London of yesterday alive for tomorrow.

Above: Tower Bridge.

Overleaf: Piccadilly Circus, Shaftesbury Avenue at night.

Right: The White Drawing Room in the staterooms, Buckingham Palace. The decor dates from the late-19th century, although the elaborate ceiling designed by Nash is of an earlier date. Most of the furniture and chandeliers came from Carlton House, the luxurious home on the Mall occupied by George IV when he was the Prince Regent. The portrait above the fireplace is of Queen Alexandra, the Danish princess who married the future Edward VII in 1862.

Left: Queen Mary's Crown (1911), which is housed with the Crown Jewels in the Tower of London.

Overleaf: Buckingham Palace.

THE ROYAL PALACES

England's kings and queens have lived in London for a thousand years and evidence of their reigns is to be found in many places. A few of their palaces may have vanished from the landscape and only local place names recall them but others survive in part or have been rebuilt and a number have withstood the passage of time and remain as elegant, or sometimes grim, reminders of the past.

The Tower of London is the oldest royal palace. Like Windsor Castle (outside the boundaries of London), it was built as a fortress to defend the city on the order of William the Conqueror at the end of the 11th century. Later kings added new towers and reception chambers, but the royal apartments have been inhabited only spasmodically. Instead, the Tower has been an armoury, a grisly prison and a place of execution. It has housed the royal menagerie and the Royal Mint, and provided secure quarters for the Crown Jewels for more than 300 years.

The Palace of Westminster was the London residence of the sovereign for 500 years but a fire in 1512 forced Henry VIII to move briefly to the Tower. Although it was rebuilt and has remained the seat of govern-

ment, neither Henry nor any subsequent monarch lived in Westminster again. Henry had inherited suburban palaces in Greenwich and in Richmond and Eltham, parts of which still stand, and the latter was in regular use until his divorce from Catherine of Aragon.

Greenwich was Henry VIII's favourite home. He was born in the great Tudor Palace of Placentia on the river's edge and two of his weddings were held there. His daughter Elizabeth I and the early Stuart sovereigns also preferred it, but during the Civil War in the 1640s Placentia fell into disrepair. Its replacement, begun by Charles II after the Restoration of the Monarchy in 1660, never became a royal residence. Instead, Charles's niece Queen Mary II and her husband William III decided

to complete it as a hospital for old sailors.

Henry VIII owned 60 houses at his death in 1547, two of which he had acquired from Cardinal Wolsey around 1530. One was in Whitehall, the other upriver at Hampton Court. Whitehall, being close to Westminster, was officially designated the king's principal seat in 1536, a position it retained for 150 years. Its days of glory came to an abrupt end in 1698 when a fire broke out. The sprawling 2,000-room palace was destroyed. Only the Banqueting House was saved. St James's Palace, the small hunting lodge which Henry VIII and Anne Boleyn had built on the edge of the park, was pressed into use as the headquarters of the Court, and to this day ambassadors are accredited to the Court of St James's.

Above: The Coronation Rings are part of the Crown Jewels in the Tower of London. The Sovereign's Ring, with a central cross of rubies, was made for William IV in 1831 and has been used at the coronation of every sovereign from Edward VII to Elizabeth II. The Queen Consort's Ring was made for Queen Adelaide, William's wife.

Opposite: Tower Green, the Tower of London. A plaque in the railed-off area of cobblestones commemorates the gruesome spot where executions took place. Two of Henry VIII's wives, Anne Boleyn and Catherine Howard, lost their heads here. A second scaffold, outside the walls of the Tower on Tower Hill, is marked by a stone in Trinity Square Gardens.

Hampton Court, Cardinal Wolsey's country home, underwent a rebuilding programme. In the 1530s Henry expended huge sums of money on an elaborate chapel, the Great Hall and splendid reception rooms. Many of the beautiful rooms remain but the present State Apartments are in the buildings designed by Christopher Wren for William and Mary.

Wren had also created magnificent rooms in Kensington Palace for the Dutch-born William and Mary, his English wife. They had bought this West London house before the destruction of Whitehall, and Kensington later became the home of Queen Anne and of George I and George II. It has since provided apartments for members of the royal family.

George III preferred Windsor and a small house in Kew Gardens. When he came to London he spent his days in the house overlooking St James's Park that he had bought for his wife, Queen Charlotte, in 1762. This was Buckingham House, the town house transformed by his son George IV into a palace. The King died before his reconstruction was finished, his brother William IV occupied the newly-built Clarence House and Buckingham Palace did not become the sovereign's official London residence until Queen Victoria moved in in 1837. It remains the principal royal palace and is the London home of Queen Elizabeth II and the Duke of Edinburgh.

Left: The Imperial State Crown. This spectacular crown, set with more than 2,800 diamonds, is worn by the sovereign after the crowning ceremony and annually at the State Opening of Parliament.

It was made for the coronation of George VI in 1937. The sapphire in the Maltese cross is said to have been taken from the finger of Edward the Confessor; the ruby is reputed to have been worn by Henry V at the Battle of Agincourt in 1415; and the diamond below it is the 317-carat Second Star of Africa, the second largest cut diamond in the world.

Above: The Palace of Westminster, better known as the Houses of Parliament. Men and women elected to Parliament sit in the House of Commons. Hereditary peers and peers appointed for life sit in the House of Lords.

Below: The Chamber of the House of Commons. Members of Parliament whose party is in power sit on the Speaker's right, members of opposition parties on the left.

Above: *The Chamber of the House of Lords.*

Left: The Royal Gallery, the Palace of Westminster. After a fire swept through the medieval palace in 1834, the Houses of Parliament were rebuilt almost entirely by the architect Sir Charles Barry whose associate Augustus Pugin was responsible for the Gothic detail and for the elaborate interiors in the House of Lords. The long fresco shows the death of Admiral Lord Nelson.

Below: The Banqueting House, Whitehall. Designed by Inigo Jones in 1619, this great reception room where masques and entertainments were held is the only significant part of the vast Stuart Palace of Whitehall to have survived a disastrous fire in 1698. The ceiling was painted by Sir Peter Paul Rubens who was paid £3,000 and rewarded with a knighthood by Charles I. The nine panels celebrate the reign of James I and the union of England and Scotland. The Banqueting House is open to the public.

Opposite above: The Fountain Court, Hampton Court Palace. Henry VIII was given Hampton Court by Cardinal Wolsey in 1529 and immediately turned it into the most magnificent palace in the land. The accession of William and Mary in 1688 brought many alterations, which Sir Christopher Wren supervised. He demolished the Tudor staterooms and the private apartments of the sovereign and designed the splendid rooms and galleries that now surround the Fountain Court. No member of the royal family occupies the palace, which is open to visitors.

Above: The Tudor Gateway, St James's Palace, is the entrance to the hunting lodge built by Henry VIII and Anne Boleyn in 1532. Early in the 18th century Sir Christopher Wren added staterooms and this small palace became the official residence of the later Stuart and Hanoverian sovereigns. To this day ambassadors are accredited to the Court of St James's, and the palace remains in royal use. The Prince of Wales has his office here and both he and the Duke and Duchess of Kent, as well as members of the royal household, occupy the private apartments. There is no public access to the palace.

Above: Kensington Palace has been a royal home since 1689 when William and Mary bought it as a country house. George II was the last sovereign to live in the palace, but the private apartments have always been used by members of the royal family. Today, the occupants include the Queen's sister, Princess Margaret and several royal princes. The staterooms are open to the public.

Left: Kew Palace. In 1773 the large brood of children born to George III and Queen Charlotte came with their tutors to study in this tiny palace in the grounds of the Royal Botanic Gardens. Later, when the education of the youngest was completed, the king and queen took up residence, and in 1818 Queen Charlotte was present in the drawing room at the marriages of two of her sons, the Duke of Clarence (William IV) and Edward, Duke of Kent (Queen Victoria's father). The palace in Kew Gardens is open.

Opposite: King William III's state bedroom in Hampton Court Palace. The state bed, with its red velvet curtains and canopy, was made for the king. The elaborate ceiling painted by Antonio Verrio shows Endymion asleep in the arms of Morpheus.

Above: Queen Elizabeth
inspecting the Yeomen of the
Guard.

Right: Windsor Castle.

Opposite: A Yeoman of the
Guard.

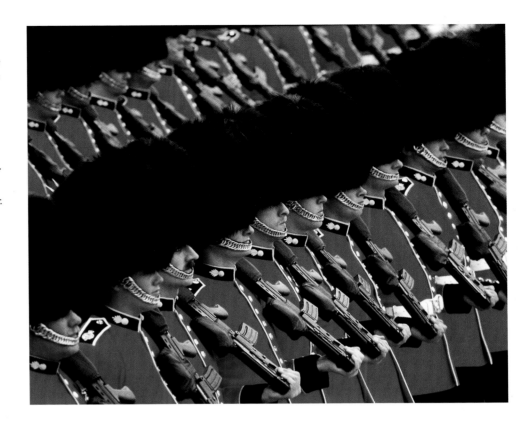

PAGEANTRY

There are few finer spectacles in the world than Queen Elizabeth II taking the salute at the ceremony of Trooping the Colour or driving in a State procession along the Mall. London's great royal pageants are unsurpassed.

London is a royal city and there are few finer spectacles than the ceremonies illustrating the relationship between Crown and State. The State Opening of Parliament, Trooping the Colour, Changing the Guard, processions along the Mall, the precision of the cavalry and foot guards and the music of military marching bands have evolved from centuries of tradition.

Whenever Queen Elizabeth II drives to a State engagement her carriage is accompanied by the Sovereign's Escort, which comprises mounted officers and men of the Household Cavalry. The soldiers, resplendent in red or blue tunics, ride gleaming black horses. The mens' tunics are overlaid with glistening steel breast-plates and white or red plumes flow from glittering helmets.

The privilege of guard-ing the sovereign belongs to the Household Division – two regiments of the Household Cavalry and five of Foot Guards. Every morning the Queen's Life Guards mount a guard in Whitehall. This ceremony follows a practice that began more than 300 years ago when 20 Life Guards were on duty at the Palace of Whitehall to protect Charles II after his return from exile in 1660. Although the palace burnt down in 1698, the guard is still changed here daily because the Horse Guards building remains the official State entrance to St James's Palace, the headquarters of the Court since the fire.

Today the sovereign resides at Buckingham Palace and the Changing of the Guard takes place on the forecourt every morning between April and July and on alternate mornings at other times. When the Queen is at home (indicated by the Royal Standard flying on the roof) three officers and 40 men make up the Guard and the Queen's colour is carried. Otherwise the number of men is reduced and the regimental colour is substituted. A detachment of the Guard marches to St James's Palace and Clarence House, where sentries are posted.

Several battalions of foot guards – the Grenadiers, Coldstream, Scots, Irish or Welsh guards – are normally stationed in London and perform the ceremony but should they be engaged elsewhere other units of the armed forces are drafted in to protect the royal palaces.

Trooping the Colour, a display of intricate marching to music, is held on Horse Guards Parade in June to

mark the sovereign's official birthday. The origin of the ceremony goes back to medieval times when the battalion's colour – a banner or flag – was marched along the ranks in order that the soldiers could recognise it as a rallying point in battle. The battalion of foot guards whose colour is being trooped is augmented by the Household Cavalry and the Massed Bands of the Household Division. The Queen takes the salute from a dais, watched by the royal dukes who are colonels of the regiments of foot guards.

Beating Retreat, held on Horse Guards Parade during the fortnight leading up to the Queen's Birthday Parade, is a centuries-old tradition that dates from a time when drums were used as military signals. The Household Division and branches of the armed forces participate in this musical display at which a member of the royal family often takes the salute.

Gun salutes are fired on special State occasions and on certain royal birthdays in either Hyde Park or Green Park by the King's Troop, the Royal Horse Artillery, who wear uniforms dating back to the 19th century. At the Tower of London the salutes are fired by the Honourable Artillery Company, a volunteer unit formed in 1537 by Henry VIII.

Not to be outdone by the pageantry in Westminster, the City of London adds a dash of colour to winter days when it stages the Lord Mayor's Show. This elaborate parade is held on the second Saturday in November when the incoming Lord Mayor, escorted by the Honourable Artillery Company, drives in the 18th-century Gold Coach from the Mansion House to the Royal Courts of Justice in the Strand. Preceding the Lord Mayor, who is elected annually, in varied coaches and on foot are the City aldermen and dignitaries in fur-trimmed gowns or gold-braided uniforms, which resemble those worn by their forebears in medieval times. The City of London may be looking towards the 21st century but it maintains traditions and the pomp and splendour of the Lord Mayor's Show with its bands and floats has altered little over the centuries.

Opposite above: A trumpeter of the Life Guards. On important ceremonial occasions trumpeters in both regiments of the Household Cavalry wear red plumes on their helmets and ride greys, rather than the black horses ridden by the remainder.

Opposite below: The Life Guards. The glistening steel cuirass breast and back plates of the Household Cavalry is the only body armour still worn by any British soldier. The present form of cuirass dates from the 1820s, and the ornamented helmet from 1842.

Left: The decorative hilt on the ceremonial sword of a Life Guard.

Overleaf: A Life Guard.

Above: The State Opening of Parliament. At the start of every new session of Parliament, Queen Elizabeth delivers a speech from the throne in the House of Lords outlining her government's proposed legislation for the forthcoming year. Although this State occasion takes place in the morning, ladies (here the Princess Royal, the Mistress of the Robes and two ladies-in-waiting on the Queen's left) wear full evening dress. Peers and peeresses also wear formal dress, their red, ermine-trimmed robes bringing added vibrancy to an already colourful ceremony.

Opposite: Carriages used in royal processions can be seen in the Royal Mews at Buckingham Palace.

Left: Guardsmen march past the Queen who takes the salute at Trooping the Colour on Horse Guards Parade.

Right: Silhouetted against the evening sky, the oversize statue of Sir Winston Churchill in Parliament Square looks towards the House of Commons, the scene of many of the wartime Prime Minister's greatest triumphs. Only one word – Churchill – is carved on the granite plinth of Ivor Roberts-Jones's bronze, which was erected in 1973.

Left top: The City of London from the South Bank.

Left centre: Henry VIII at Madame Tussaud's and interior of Victoria and Albert Museum.

Left below: Tower Bridge.

LONDON SIGHTS

St Paul's Cathedral, Tower Bridge, Big Ben and Trafalgar Square are instantly recognisable sights that symbolise London. Each one is among the familiar buildings and monuments visible from the top of a bus, which Gladstone, the Victorian prime minister, said was the best way to see London.

A large number of the best-known sights are concentrated in the City and the West End, within a short distance of the river between Tower Bridge and Lambeth Bridge. Many of them can be seen from the pleasure boats that cruise the Thames. Others are farther afield in Chelsea, Kensington, Greenwich, Hampstead, Richmond or Docklands. While these are all places most visitors wish to see, other districts should not be ignored: each area of London yields strange and rewarding pleasures, especially to the explorer who prefers to walk.

A tour of Central London on a bus will pass the Tower of London, City churches, the Mansion House, Piccadilly Circus, Nelson's Column and the squares and important buildings of the West End as well as some of the royal parks. Yet the view through Admiralty Arch,

along the Mall, to Buckingham Palace and the bright lights of Leicester Square can be seen only by those on foot. The splendid neo-Gothic features of the Houses of Parliament, the majestic bridges and the solemn entrance through Traitors' Gate to the Tower of London can be glimpsed from a bus but the best views are from the river.

The sights and pleasures of London do not always reveal themselves to people in a hurry. Look up, look down to see stone carvings high on a City church or an epitaph on a great man's tomb. Hidden treasures can be discovered only by looking around. Time is needed to appreciate the tiny galleons sailing down the Mall on the top of the lamp posts, to admire the elaborately decorated benches on the Embankment or the ornamental signs hanging outside pubs or

historic companies. The architectural curiosities at the end of narrow alleys, the unusual species of trees in the royal parks or the rare wildfowl swimming on the lakes can be discovered only by those who seek them out.

Nor should visitors ignore the interiors of public buildings or famous attractions such as the futuristic "virtual reality theme park" in the Trocadero Centre or the waxworks in Madame Tussaud's. They are fascinating. Experience the Whispering Gallery in St Paul's Cathedral and from it admire the artist James Thornhill's painting of the dome and details of the ironwork and carving, which cannot be appreciated from the nave. In the crypt lies the black marble sarcophagus in which Admiral Lord Nelson is buried but a more personal image of the naval victor, dressed in some of his own clothes, is conveyed in the life-size wax effigy in the undercroft of Westminster Abbey. Waxwork models of contemporary heroes, of pop stars, football players, the royal family and infamous as well as celebrated personalities attract crowds to Madame Tussaud's but the marble statues and memorials to distinguished people in the Abbey, especially those in Poets' Corner, are also a great draw.

Almost three million people annually head down-river to Greenwich to see the world's prime meridian line – longitude zero – at the Old Royal Observatory. They go to the Royal Naval College on the site of a Tudor palace and to the Queen's House, the Palladian-style villa in which Charles II's mother, Henrietta Maria, lived in 1660. Some continue down-stream to see the Thames Barrier, "the eighth wonder of the world", or cross into Docklands to look at the new commercial developments and the revitalised deep water docks around Canary Wharf. Others travel upriver to Kew to walk among the exotic trees and plants in the Royal Botanic Gardens. They go to Richmond to see the remains of a royal palace, the town's Georgian aspects and to gaze at the splendid prospect from the hill before journeying farther upstream to Hampton Court and on to Windsor.

A steep climb to the viewing platform of the 202 ft Monument, the City's memorial to the Great Fire of 1666, or a lift-ride up the slender 284 ft campanile of Westminster Cathedral pro-vide wide and striking views. They afford a perspective of London that few people realise they can enjoy.

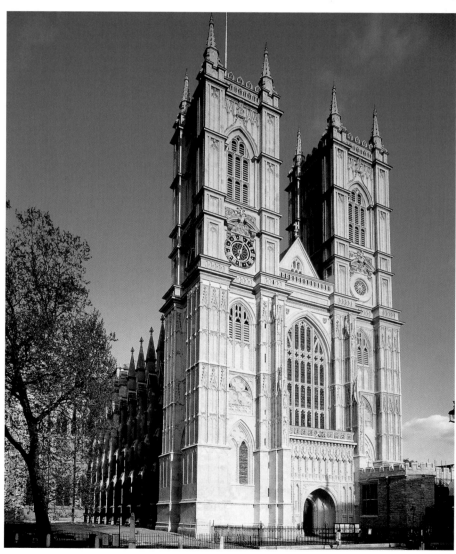

Above: *The west front of Westminster Abbey. The abbey, built by King Edward the Confessor, was consecrated in December 1065, ten days before the king's death. A year later, on Christmas Day, William the Conqueror became the first king of England to be crowned in the church, since when every sovereign, except Edward V and Edward VIII, has been crowned here.*

The Confessor's abbey was rebuilt in the 13th and 14th centuries by Henry III and Richard II. The western end remained unfinished until the architect Nicholas Hawksmoor designed the twin pinnacled towers early in the 18th century. Sixteen monarchs are buried in the abbey. They include Edward the Confessor, Elizabeth I and her grandfather Henry VII, who was responsible for the magnificent chapel that bears his name. Its lace-like fan-vaulting, groined arches and the stone carvings of saints are the finest examples of early Tudor workmanship.

Above: The impressive nave of Westminster Abbey is the highest in England. The vaulting is studded with golden bosses and 16 Waterford glass chandeliers hang from the sides. These were given by the Guinness family in 1965 to celebrate the 900th anniversary of the abbey. In the foreground is the Grave of the Unknown Warrior, and the aisles and transepts are filled with monuments and memorials to the great and the good.

Previous page: The Palace of Westminster, more familiarly known as the Houses of Parliament. Westminster Hall, in the centre with the deep roof, was built by William Rufus in 1097. It was part of the medieval palace of the sovereigns, and has the finest oak hammerbeam ceiling in Europe. Amazingly, the hall has survived two major fires, one in 1512 and another in 1834, which resulted in the present surrounding buildings.

Above, left and opposite: For many people the most distinctive feature of the Houses of Parliament is the clock tower, or Big Ben as it is more usually called. Properly speaking, the name derives from the great bell whose chimes are broadcast all over the world by the BBC. How it acquired the name is uncertain. It may have been as a compliment to Sir Benjamin Hall, the Commissioner of Works, or called after "Big Ben" Caunt, a popular 42-year-old boxer, who shortly before the bell was installed in 1858, went 60 rounds in a heavyweight fight.

Above: St Paul's Cathedral was built by Sir Christopher Wren in a classical Renaissance style to replace the Gothic cathedral destroyed in the Great Fire of 1666. Work began in 1675 and, unlike Bramante and Michelangelo in Rome, Wren was still alive in 1710 when his masterpiece was completed. Until modern times the great dome dominated the London skyline.

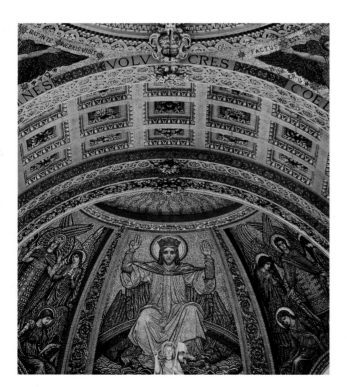

Opposite: The Choir and High Altar of St Paul's Cathedral. The altar designed by Wren was replaced in the 1880s and again after the Second World War when one of the few bombs to fall on St Paul's shattered it. The present altar with its imposing baldachino is dedicated to the 335,451 men and women of the Commonwealth who gave their lives in two world wars. The wooden choir stalls are by Grinling Gibbons, the Flemish craftsman employed by Wren.

Right: The top of Nelson's Column. Seven years after the creation of Trafalgar Square a letter to The Times *suggested it would be a suitable place to honour Admiral Lord Nelson. The statue of the victor at the Battle of Trafalgar was paid for by public subscription and hoisted onto the top of the Corinthian column in November 1843. Contrary to popular belief, Nelson is not wearing an eye-patch. The total height is 170 ft.*

Below: Trafalgar Square looking south towards Whitehall and the Houses of Parliament. The square, part of a plan by John Nash, was laid out on the site of the former royal mews in 1830 and the National Gallery opened shortly afterwards on the north side. Nelson's Column's came later.*

Above: *Piccadilly Circus was laid out in 1819 by the architect John Nash as a* rond point *on a grand processional thoroughfare from the Prince Regent's exotic house on the Mall to a proposed palace in Regent's Park. In the event, Carlton House was demolished and the palace never built. The name Piccadilly comes from the word "pickadill", a shirt frill. These were made in a nearby house early in the 17th century.*

Left: *A memorial fountain topped by a statue of Eros was erected in Piccadilly Circus in 1893 as a tribute to the philanthrophic 7th Earl of Shaftesbury, after whom nearby Shaftesbury Avenue is named. The sculptor Alfred Gilbert symbolised the earl's charitable work for the poor by creating a figure of "Love sending forth indiscriminately, yet with purpose, his missiles of kindness...". The metal is aluminium, the first time it had been used for a statue.*

Right: St Mary-le-Bow, Cheapside. Apart from its crypt, the Norman church of St Mary-le-Bow, in Cheapside was destroyed in 1666 but when Wren rebuilt it he incorporated the crypt and he placed balustrades above the square tower to commemorate the balcony from which Edward III and Queen Philippa had watched tournaments in the 14th century. Legend insists that anyone born within the sound of Bow Bells is a Cockney or true Londoner.

Left: St Bride's, Fleet Street, was designed by Christopher Wren in the aftermath of the Great Fire of 1666. The spire is said to have inspired a baker on nearby Ludgate Hill to create tiered wedding cakes, a bride's cake. For centuries the church has been associated with print and printers and until recently Britain's newspapers had their head offices in the district. Although the newspapers have moved to other parts of London, St Bride's retains close links with the press.

Left: St Bartholomew the Great, Smithfield, was built as an Augustinian priory in the first decade of the 12th century by Rahere, Henry I's court jester. Parts of this massive parish church deteriorated in the 18th century and chapels not in use were rented out: in 1724 Benjamin Franklin, the eminent American scientist and diplomat, worked in a print shop in the Lady Chapel.

Below: Westminster Cathedral is the leading Roman Catholic church in England and Wales. Designed in 1895 by John Francis Bentley in an Italianate-Byzantine style, the vast basilica immediately invited criticism: one important Catholic thought it "a megalomaniac hulk in a sea of unsightliness" and wags christened the 284 ft campanile "the Roman candle". The marble and mosaic decoration of the interior, begun at the time of the consecration in 1903, is slowly being completed.

The Chapel Royal, Hampton Court Palace. The chapel built by Cardinal Wolsey was subsequently embellished by Henry VIII who was responsible for the installation of the magnificent, blue ceiling with shimmering stars and gilded pendants. The oak reredos, carved by Grinling Gibbons, and later decorations between the windows were designed by Christopher Wren.

St George's Chapel, Windsor, is a splendid example of perpendicular architecture. The chapel was begun by Edward IV in 1477 and the exquisite vaulting in the nave added by

Henry VII. The banner of each Knight or Lady of the Garter, England's highest order of chivalry, hangs above his or her stall in the choir.

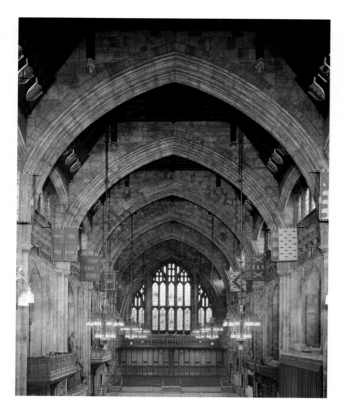

Above left: *The Great Hall, Guildhall. Since the 12th century the City of London has been administered from Guildhall and its system of government was adopted by Parliament. With the Lord Mayor presiding from the dais, and with aldermen and sheriffs in attendance, the Common Councilmen elected by 26 City wards meet twice monthly with officials of the Corporation of the City of London to conduct the affairs of the "square mile".*

Part of the walls of the Great Hall built in 1411 survived the Great Fire of London in 1666, and discoloured stones can be seen in the medieval columns. After further damage by enemy action during the Second World War, the hall was restored and the roof reconstructed.

Above: *The Egyptian Hall, the Mansion House. The Lord Mayor of London's official residence was designed in the middle of the 18th century in "the Egyptian manner". The hall is used for large banquets and receptions.*

Opposite: *"The Room", Lloyds of London. Somewhat incongruously, a room designed more than 200 years ago by Robert Adam for a house in Wiltshire has been reconstructed on the 11th gallery of the controversial, surrealistic glass and steel structure that Richard Rogers designed in the early 1980s for the world's foremost insurance market.*

Left: *Lloyds of London.*

Left: The Royal Courts of Justice, Strand. The country's principal law courts for hearing civil cases are in this pinnacled Gothic structure, which Queen Victoria opened in 1882.

Below: The Bank of England. The central bank of the country was founded in 1694 to raise money during the French-Dutch war. The present ten-storey building, put up between 1921 and 1937, incorporated the windowless curtain wall of Sir John Soane's late-18th-century bank.

Above: The Grand Hall of the Old Bailey, or to give it its official title, the Central Criminal Court. The great domed court building in which many of the country's more notorious cases are brought to trial, stands on the site of Newgate Prison, an infamous place of incarceration and execution. The prison was demolished in 1902 and rebuilt using some of the old stone. The marble grandeur of the hall is in stern contrast to the sleazy, unpleasant crimes that are revealed in the courtrooms.

Above: Marble Arch. John Nash's arch is based on the Arch of Constantine in Rome. Constructed as a triumphal entrance to Buckingham Palace. The equestrian statue of George IV, today in Trafalgar Square, was originally intended to surmount the arch.

vas erected on the palace forecourt in 1828 but 22 years later, when the east front of the palace was built, it was removed to Hyde Park.

Above: Tower Bridge. The most recognisable bridge in London celebrated its centenary in 1994. The twin towers, their medieval style complementing the Tower of London, are linked by a glassed-in walkway 140 ft above the Thames and by twin bascules on the road which are raised and lowered to allow ships to sail through. The bridge forms the eastern boundary of the City of London and is one of four City bridges that are no charge on the public purse. Medieval City merchants grateful for the trade brought to them centuries ago by London Bridge, then the only river crossing, left money "for God and the bridge". The income from this fund has since built and maintained the bridges linking the City and the south bank of the river.

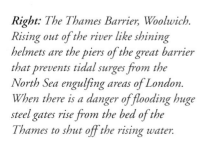

Right: The Thames Barrier, Woolwich. Rising out of the river like shining helmets are the piers of the great barrier that prevents tidal surges from the North Sea engulfing areas of London. When there is a danger of flooding huge steel gates rise from the bed of the Thames to shut off the rising water.

Left: St Katharine's Docks. Immediately downriver from Tower Bridge, the dock was created in 1825 on the site of a medieval hospice. The dock was the main import area for tea, spices, wine and ivory. Following closure in 1968, a major redevelopment was put in hand. The Ivory House was restored, an "olde worlde" pub was reconstructed and a once-shabby area was transformed into a lively yacht basin.

Left: The Millennium Dome. The centre of the world's millennium celebrations and a new London landmark for the 21st century.

Right: Canary Wharf is the centrepiece of the redeveloped area that formed London's docks in previous centuries. Completed in the early 1990s, the tower rises to a height of 800 ft, making it currently the tallest building in Britain.

Left: The Royal Naval College, Greenwich. Greenwich has the finest architectural buildings in England. The Tudor palace, the favourite home of Henry VIII and Queen Elizabeth I, was demolished and replaced by the present palatial complex that was first a hospital for veteran sailors and then a naval college.

The small white building set back from the river is the Queen's House, the first classical domestic building in England, which Inigo Jones designed in 1616.

On the hill above lies the Old Royal Observatory, built by Wren in 1675 for John Flamsteed, the first Astronomer Royal. The complex was declared a World Heritage Site in 1997.

Right: Detail on the gates of the Royal Naval College, Greenwich. Known originally as Greenwich Hospital, the celebrated buildings were home to thousands of old sailors until 1869. Four years later the Admiralty moved the Royal Naval College from Portsmouth to Greenwich. It became a college for officers of all three defence forces but this use ceased when the college was decommissioned in 1997.

Right: The 24-hour clock at the Old Royal Observatory, Greenwich. The world's prime meridian line, longitude zero, runs through the observatory from where time around the world has been calculated since 1884.

Opposite: The Painted Hall in the Royal Naval College. This triumphant example of interior decoration is one of London's few achievements in the grand baroque manner. The artist James Thornhill spent 19 years painting the allegorical ceiling and walls which celebrate the reigns of William and Mary and of George I. The hall was a dining room for officers of the armed forces who came to Greenwich on study courses. The Painted Hall and the Chapel are open to the public.

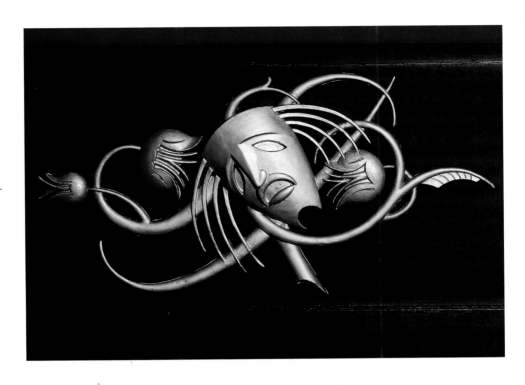

CITY OF THE ARTS

London has a lively mixture of visual and performing arts. More buildings are devoted to displaying artefacts from the past, to the endeavours of artists and to productions of drama, dance, opera and music than in any other capital city. Little wonder that London has been acclaimed as "the cultural capital of the world".

Spread across the metropolis are more than 250 museums and art galleries, and hundreds of smaller commercial galleries. Collections of antiquities, fine arts and scientific apparatus are explained and exhibited within large museums such as the British Museum, the Victoria and Albert Museum and the Science Museum. There is so much to see and do in the great institutions that repeat visits are needed. Many of the cultural palaces are designed to have wide appeal to all age groups. Others, such as the Museum of London, which illustrates the story of the capital, or the National Army Museum, cater for particular interests.

The National Gallery, with its assembly of Old Masters, and the Tate Gallery, where only a proportion of its vast holding of 19th- and 20th-century paintings and sculpture can be shown,

should also be seen many times. But smaller, lesser-known museums and art galleries are just as rewarding. In Lincoln's Inn Fields, the extraordinary curiosities, architectural drawings and paintings by Hogarth left to the nation in 1837 by the architect Sir John Soane should not be missed. Nor should the Wallace Collection in Manchester Square, which has splendid pictures, among them Frans Hal's *The Laughing Cavalier*, superb miniatures, French porcelain and furniture. Caricatures in the National Museum of Cartoon Art in Whitechapel raise a laugh and surgical instruments in the Old Operating Theatre at London Bridge send shivers down the spine.

London theatre is the envy of the world and the curtain goes up nightly in more than 40 playhouses in the West End and on the

stages of the Royal National Theatre and the Royal Shakespeare Company. Productions of classics are interspersed with modern plays and large-scale musicals. Distinguished actors appear in comedies and dramas, and often a great star is to be found in a fringe theatre, lured there by the chance to perform a certain play.

Opera on a grand scale is heard in the Royal Opera House, Covent Garden, and the London Coliseum. The Royal Opera shares its gilded premises with the Royal Ballet, and at the Coliseum, when the English National Opera is on tour, international dance companies and English National Ballet take up residence.

London has a number of international orchestras: the London Symphony Orchestra is based in the Barbican Centre; others play in the

Right: The Natural History Museum is one of a number of museums built in South Kensington on land acquired with the profits of the Great Exhibition of 1851. Many of its early natural history and botanical collections formed the nucleus of the British Museum when it opened in 1759 but these were moved from Bloomsbury when the brick and terracotta Romanesque building was completed in 1881. The dinosaurs, skeletons of large mammals, stuffed birds and butterflies are especially popular with children. The museum is also an important research centre.

Royal Festival Hall and the Royal Albert Hall. The Wigmore Hall offers chamber concerts and recitals and many of the City churches have lunchtime music programmes; jazz, rock, pop, reggae and folk music abound in clubs and pubs, and the occasional megastar sings in the vast reaches of Wembley.

The cultural renaissance that has gripped London in the 1990s is scheduled to continue. Schemes are afloat for any number of museums, art galleries and theatres. The British Museum is setting up a World Textile Centre and roofing over the Great Court around the Reading Room. The new British Library rises over St Pancras. The Victoria and Albert Museum is considering a futuristic extension. The National Maritime Museum has embarked on a reconstruction of the Neptune Hall, and the Science Museum is building a wing devoted to contemporary science, medicine and technology.

In theatreland, the Royal Opera House is putting up a multi-million pound extension. A new Sadler's Wells Theatre is rising from the ashes of the cradle in which the Royal Ballet, English National Opera and the Royal National Theatre were nurtured. And the Lyceum Theatre, out of use for 57 years, has been resurrected.

Renewal on the South Bank, fast becoming the cultural heart of London, is forging ahead. A redundant power station is being converted to hold the Tate Gallery's collection of 20th-century art. The National Film Theatre is installing a giant IMAX screen in the bullring at Waterloo. A major refurbishment of the Royal National Theatre has been undertaken and Shakespeare's plays are being performed in the Globe Theatre, a reconstruction of his 17th-century wooden "O". London has a flourishing arts scene.

Above: Sir John Soane Museum, Lincoln's Inn Fields. One of the forgotten gems of London, this enchanting museum contains antiquities, paintings, statuary and furniture collected by John Soane, the architect of the late-18th-century Bank of England. The paintings include Hogarth's series The Rake's Progress *and*
The Election, *etchings by Piranesi and among the architectural drawings are almost 9,000 by the Adam brothers. Soane left his house to the nation, stipulating that it should be kept "as nearly as possible in the state" in which it was left at his death in 1837. Little has altered.*

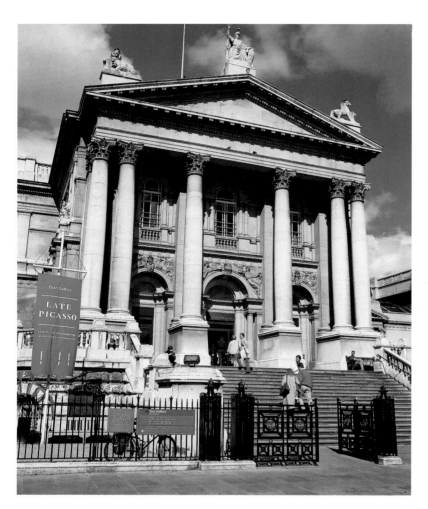

Left: The Tate Gallery houses the British national collection of modern art as well as paintings and sculpture by major British artists of the 18th and 19th centuries. Works by British artists such as Hogarth, Reynolds and Constable, by internationally renowned Impressionists, Post-Impressionists and representatives of movements such as Cubism and Dadaism are to be found on the walls of the lofty, spacious galleries. The priceless collection of paintings and drawings by J. M. W. Turner are in a purpose-built extension, and plans are in progress to show a far wider survey of the gallery's 20th-century holdings in the disused powerhouse on the South Bank in Southwark.

Opposite: The Sainsbury Wing, the National Gallery. Opened in 1991, the extension contains the early Renaissance collection. The church-like enfilade stretches from the 19th-century main building, where the national collection of masterpieces hang. Like the British Museum and the Tate Gallery, the National Gallery is one of the most visited places in London.

Right: The Reading Room, the British Museum. This wonderful circular room with a dome which is one of the widest in the world is the centrepiece of the museum, although few of the six million people who come to see the antiquities and art are able to visit it as until it closed in 1997 it was reserved for users of the British Library, a separate independent body since 1973. With the removal of the library to St Pancras, the museum is able to reclaim the room where Karl Marx and many famous men studied, and plans to expand and create exciting new facilities in the Reading Room are forging ahead.

Opposite: "The Last Night of the Proms" takes place in the Royal Albert Hall in mid-September at the end of the eight-week season of annual promenade concerts founded by Sir Henry Wood in 1895. "Music for the people at a price the people can afford" was his aim and in 1996, for the first time, more than 25,000 people attended a live performance in Hyde Park and then joined the 5,500 people in the hall by watching the final concert on large screens.

Above: The Royal Albert Hall, Kensington. Concerts, pageants, meetings, dances and tennis tournaments are held in this enormous hall built as a memorial to Queen Victoria's husband, Prince Albert.

Right: The Theatre Royal, Haymarket. With its elegant Georgian façade and warm old-gold auditorium, it is easy to appreciate why most actors love this theatre, which is also a great favourite with playgoers. The theatre was designed by John Nash in 1820.

Left: Wyndham's Theatre. Many of the theatres in the West End date from the turn of the century when elaborate decoration was the fashion. Wyndham's, built for the impresario Charles Wyndham and his wife, the actress Mary Moore, has ceiling paintings in the manner of François Boucher. The portraits above the proscenium arch are of the playwrights Richard Brinsley Sheridan and Oliver Goldsmith.

Opposite: The Palace Theatre was an opera house when it opened in 1891. It was later a variety hall, and the ballerina Pavlova danced on its stage before the First World War. It had a short period as a cinema but reverted to the home of large-scale musical comedies in the 1920s. Tim Rice and Andrew Lloyd-Webber's Jesus Christ Superstar *played here throughout the 1970s and Lloyd-Webber subsequently bought the theatre, in which musicals remain top of the bill.*

Right: The magnificent red and gilded horseshoe auditorium of the Royal Opera House, Covent Garden. The huge theatre is home to two companies – the Royal Opera and the Royal Ballet. The present theatre, dating from 1858 and the third on the site, is undergoing major alterations scheduled to finish before the millennium.

Overleaf: Leicester Square could happily be renamed Entertainment Square. Four major cinemas with a total of 20 screens overlook the small park which has strategically placed busts and statues of famous London residents, among them Shakespeare, Sir Joshua Reynolds and Sir Charles Chaplin. All around the square on fine evenings street performers entertain the crowds in the square or outside the restaurants.

LIFE AND LEISURE

Life in London differs little from anywhere else. The daily routine of work, rest and play is much the same as in any other city. But a subtle change occurs where leisure is concerned. London has an energy and excitement unmatched by few other capitals. It is the "coolest" city in the world, according to US media reports, which have compared the Nineties to the Swinging Sixties.

This is due, in part, to the huge growth of restaurants and nightclubs, to popular fashion and to the entertainment available in this cosmopolitan city. Multi-ethnic cooking styles, trendy clothes and a thriving music scene reflect the cultural diversity of modern London. Cosmopolitanism has ensured that the famous department stores, such as Harrods, Harvey Nichols and Selfridges, cater for a widespread clientele. And fashionable designer clothes and speciality goods produced by smaller firms are sought after. However, not all the big stores and boutiques are concentrated in the West End or Knightsbridge. Many have branches in the new shopping malls in the suburbs.

Even street markets have their specialities. Covent Garden, once London's principal fruit, flower and vegetable market, today has a central bazaar area with stalls selling antiques, clothes, arts and crafts, and shops and restaurants overlooking the piazza. Butchers and fishmongers in Leadenhall Market in the City sell game, poultry and fish, as they have done for six centuries. In the East End, around Brick Lane, and in Southall in West London the provisions have an Eastern or Oriental flavour. Antiques are on stalls in Portobello Road, near Notting Hill Gate. Flowers and plants fill the market in Columbia Road. Silver is the speciality in the New Caledonian Market in Bermondsey. Greenwich's covered market is devoted to arts and crafts. And traders around Camden Lock sell all kinds of everything from clothes and jewellery to bric-a-brac.

Many shops and street markets are as well-known as the more solid historic sights but a few familiar London icons are disappearing as new brooms sweep away traditions considered outmoded. Red livery is no longer de rigueur for the capital's buses. Not all taxi cabs are black anymore, and the celebrated red telephone boxes have largely been replaced by steel and perspex booths.

But some things never change. Despite a proposal to prevent people feeding the pigeons in Trafalgar Square, no one can stop the birds landing around the fountains or on Landseer's bronze lions. Artists, some with work of questionable quality, still line the railings along Piccadilly with paintings on Sundays and orators fired by passionate causes continue to deliver rousing messages from soapboxes at Speakers' Corner in Hyde Park. And the parks, the people's pleasure grounds, remain as popular with Londoners as with visitors who come to admire the rose beds and floral displays, or simply to sit or play on the lawns.

The annual social and sporting calendar has altered little during the 20th century. The Chelsea Flower Show in the grounds of the Royal Hospital and the Summer Exhibition at the Royal Academy of Arts in Piccadilly herald the start of "the season". Wimbledon is still the best tennis championships in the world. Cricket teams from Australia, the West Indies and Commonwealth countries bring crowds to watch the test matches at Lords and the Oval. Football fans have fixtures at Wembley, and the stands at famous clubs, such as Arsenal or Chelsea, are normally packed with spectators on match days.

On the Thames the Doggett's Coat and Badge Race, rowed annually each July since 1715 from London Bridge to Chelsea by apprentice watermen, attracts thousands. Crowds are even larger when the Oxford versus Cambridge Boat Race is rowed from Putney to Mortlake in the spring, a challenge that has been taking place since 1829.

The most recent changes in the leisure arena in London have been the proliferation of quality restaurants and trendy nightclubs. Deciding where to eat poses problems: Italian, Indian or Irish, English, Viennese or American? The choice is bewildering, as indeed it is when it comes to music. Pubs with a theme and a plethora of clubs offer everything from jazz, soul, funk and jungle to laid back break-beat and rock. No one can say that London does not have vitality.

Opposite: Jazz musicians entertain customers at a London pub.

Above: Trafalgar Square is a traditional rallying place at all times of year. Every day visitors to London come to feed the pigeons or climb onto the lions beneath Nelson's Column, and on important sporting occasions supporters gather here to celebrate or commiserate. In the weeks leading up to Christmas carol singers are to be heard under the Christmas tree and on New Year's Eve thousands gather to welcome in the New Year.

Left: Newspapers, especially the evening paper, are sold on street corners, in doorways and outside stations by vendors. The newsvendor is a traditional and familiar sight in the centre of the city.

Overleaf: Chinatown in Soho, Knightsbridge store window.

Above, right, below: St James's Park, the prettiest of London's royal parks, is overlooked by a number of royal houses. A curving lake inhabited by many species of wildfowl flows through the centre. On fine summer days workers from government offices in Whitehall relax under the magnificent specimen trees and admire the carefully-tended flower beds. A number of railed off areas are specially reserved for rare birds and wildfowl, though it is doubtful that they can read the notices informing them so!

Above: The Sunken Garden at Kensington Palace was laid out in Edwardian days as a reminder of Queen Anne's early-18th-century formal garden. It is planted with a varied array of colourful flowers throughout the year.

Above: *Little Venice, Maida Vale. The Grand Union Canal, which links London to Birmingham,*
encircles the northern edge of Regent's Park. Houseboats, restaurants and barges ferrying
visitors are a regular sight between Little Venice and Camden Lock.

Left: The Pond Garden at Hampton Court Palace contains the brightest of flowers from spring to autumn. The tulips, hyacinths and wallflowers that provide a riot of colour early in the year give way in summer to stocks, zinnias, geraniums, dahlias and African marigolds. The castellated red brick building on the river's edge is William III's Banqueting House.

Below: Chelsea Physic Garden is, after Oxford, the oldest existing botanical garden in England. It was first planted in 1673 by the Society of Apothecaries and "the collection of innumerable rarities" that the 17th-century diarist John Evelyn noted has always been of great interest to botanists and specialist gardeners.

Above: Sunday in the Park. The railings along Green Park, on Piccadilly, become a free art gallery on Sundays when paintings of questionable quality are hung by artists hoping to tempt visitors in search of a souvenir.

Above: Signs outside public houses often commemorate battles, famous military commanders, well known personalities or, in this case, a sailing ship.

Right: Stalls selling antiques outside the shops and pubs in the Portobello Road attract bargain hunters, specially on Saturdays.

Above: *Speakers' Corner. Orators on soap boxes at the Marble Arch end of Hyde Park assail the crowd with reactionary views on public, political and religious issues on Sundays.*

Opposite: Harrods. The outline of London's best known store is picked out in tiny lights at night. Inside visitors are invited "to enter a different world". The store has grown from a small grocery shop opened in 1849 to a massive, world famous emporium with departments selling a huge variety of merchandise.

Opposite (inset): The Food Halls, Harrods. Many of the departments in this large store have been transformed in recent years into a glittering Mecca for shoppers and the Food Halls, which are the heart of the store, have been restored to their Edwardian splendour.

Above: Covent Garden Market. Today, stalls selling antiques, clothes and arts and crafts occupy the market where fruit and vegetables were sold for more than 300 years. The produce market moved across the Thames to Nine Elms in 1974. The covered market of 1830 was then restored, the surrounding area revitalised and nowadays street entertainers attract passers-by throughout the day, some performers in the Piazza giving Punch and Judy shows similar to the one the diarist Samuel Pepys saw there in May 1662.

Below: Selfridge's, the largest department store in Oxford Street, was opened in 1909 by Gordon Selfridge, an American. The imaginative Christmas window displays always attract large crowds.

Above: Many of the much-loved 1930s red telephone boxes have been replaced by more modern glass and steel structures, but a few remain and have been granted the same status as important listed buildings by English Heritage.

Above: Black cabs are a familiar sight all over London. When the yellow light is switched on the taxi is available for hire.

Right: The familiar logo that indicates one of London's transport facilities, in this instance an underground station. Similar circles on poles in the street signal bus stops.

Left: Red buses are synonymous with London, but times are changing and lines such as this one in Oxford Street are increasingly rare since the liveries of private companies have been allowed.

Right: The familiar Routemaster bus with the open platform at the rear is slowly being phased out, replaced by one-man buses.

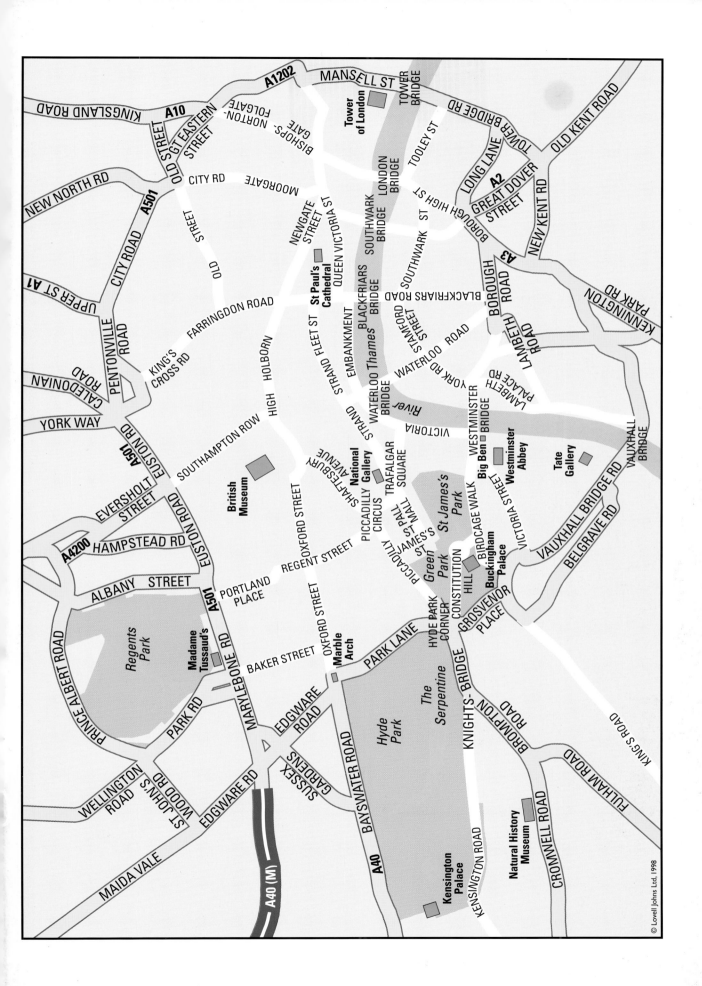

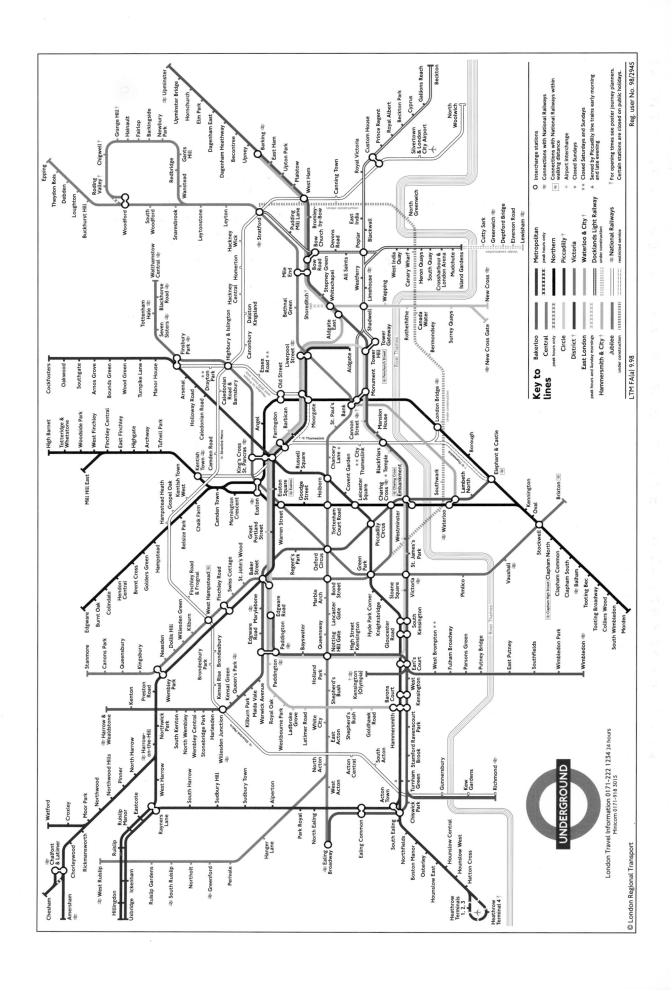